S0-AQD-946

Company's Coming
PINT SIZE BOOKS
By Jean Paré
BUFFETS

Company's Coming
PINT SIZE BOOKS
By Jean Paré
PARTY PLANNING

Company's Coming
PINT SIZE BOOKS
By Jean Paré
FINGER FOOD

EASY ENTERTAINING • BOOK ONE

Double Dill Dip
Double the pleasure. A treat with veggies.

500 mL	2 cups	Sour cream
125 g	4 oz.	Cream cheese, softened
10 mL	2 tsp.	Parsley flakes
2 mL	½ tsp.	Garlic powder
10 mL	2 tsp.	Onion flakes
5 mL	1 tsp.	Onion salt
10 mL	2 tsp.	Lemon juice
375 mL	1½ tsp.	Dill weed

Combine first 8 ingredients in blender. Blend smooth. Turn into bowl.

Jar of pickled dill tidbits, drained
Fresh dill, for garnish

Stir in dill bits. Garnish with dill. Makes 4½ cups (1.05 L) dip.

Dippers
Assorted fresh vegetables: strips of carrot, green, red or yellow pepper, celery, cauliflower and broccoli florets, mushrooms or Cheese Thins, page 61.

Arrange around or beside bowl of dip.

Pictured below.

Cheese Thins
Large thin wafers that are crispy good. Makes showy basketful.

500 mL	2 cups	All purpose flour
250 mL	1 cup	Grated sharp Cheddar cheese
15 mL	1 tbsp.	Granulated sugar
2 mL	½ tsp.	Baking soda
2 mL	½ tsp.	Salt
0.5 mL	⅛ tsp.	Onion powder
		Cayenne pepper
60 mL	¼ cup	Cooking oil
125 mL	½ cup	Water

Measure first 7 ingredients into bowl. Stir well.

Add cooking oil and water. Mix until you can form a ball. Cover and let stand 20 minutes. Divide into 4 portions. Roll 1 portion paper thin on lightly floured surface. Cut into 8 wedges. Arrange on ungreased baking sheet. Bake in 375°F (190°C) oven for about 10 minutes until crisp and browned. Repeat for remaining dough. Repeat for wedges. Serve with Double Dill Dip, page 60. Makes 32 wedges.

Pictured on this page.

Small Indulgences...

SAUTÉED CABBAGE

An economical vegetable. It has a very faint hint of sauerkraut flavor.

Chopped or sliced onion	½ cup	175 mL
Water	¾ cup	175 mL
Grated cabbage, packed	4 cups	900 mL
Vegetable cooking oil	1 tbsp.	15 mL
Vinegar	1 tbsp.	15 mL

Combine onion and water in frying pan. Simmer until soft.
Add cabbage. Stir. Add more water if needed. Cover. Simmer about 6 minutes until cabbage is tender crisp.
Add cooking oil and vinegar. Stir-fry about 20 to 25 minutes until cabbage is browned and water has boiled away. Makes 2 cups (450 mL).

¼ cup/125 mL contains:	
Energy	61 Calories (254 kJ)
Cholesterol	0 mg
Sodium	14 mg
Fat	4 g

Taste the Tradition

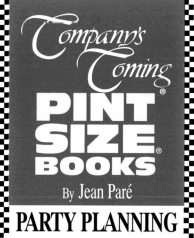

Company's Coming

PINT SIZE BOOKS

By Jean Paré

PARTY PLANNING

Eighth Printing August 1996

ISBN 1-895455-26-X

Published and Distributed by
Company's Coming Publishing Limited
Box 8037, Station "F"
Edmonton, Alberta, Canada
T6H 4N9

**Published Simultaneously in
Canada and the United States of America**

Front and Back Cover Photo

1. Tossed Salad page 13
2. Punch Sparkler page 18
3. Citrus Ice Ring page 16
4. Marble Cheesecake page 12
5. Tomato Rose page 11
6. Shrimp Mousse page 10
7. Party Flower Napkins page 17

Dishware Courtesy Of: The Bay China Department
Table Linen Courtesy Of: Ashbrook's

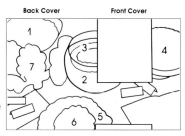

Printed In Canada

The Jean Paré Story

Jean Paré grew up understanding that the combination of family, friends and home cooking is the essence of a good life. When she left home she took with her many acquired family recipes, her love of cooking and her intriguing desire to read recipe books like novels! While raising a family of four, Jean was always busy in her kitchen preparing delicious, tasty treats and savory meals for family and friends of all ages. Her reputation flourished as the mom who would happily feed the neighborhood.

In 1963, when her children had all reached school age, Jean volunteered to cater to the 50th anniversary of the Vermilion School of Agriculture, now Lakeland College, in the town of Vermilion, Alberta, Canada. Working out of her home, Jean prepared a dinner for over 1000 people which launched a flourishing catering operation that continued for over eighteen years. During that time she was provided with countless opportunities to test new ideas with immediate feedback – resulting in empty plates and contented customers! Whether preparing cocktail sandwiches for a house party or serving a hot meal for 1500 people, Jean Paré earned a reputation for good food, courteous service and reasonable prices.

"Why don't you write a cookbook?" Time and again, as requests for her recipes mounted, Jean was asked that question. Jean's response was to team up with her son Grant Lovig in the fall of 1980 to form Company's Coming Publishing Limited. April 14, 1981, marked the debut of "150 DELICIOUS SQUARES", the first Company's Coming cookbook in what soon would become Canada's most popular cookbook series. By 1995, sales had surpassed ten million cookbooks.

Company's Coming cookbooks are now distributed throughout Canada, the United States and numerous overseas markets, all under the guidance of Jean's daughter, Gail Lovig. The series is published in English and French, plus a Spanish edition is available in Mexico. In 1993 Company's Coming began producing the smaller, more specialized PINT SIZE series of cookbooks which continue to reflect the familiar and trusted style of Company's Coming. Soon a variety of other new formats will be available in addition to the bestselling soft cover series.

Jean Paré's approach to cooking has always called for quick and easy recipes using everyday ingredients. She continues to gain new supporters by adhering to what she calls "the golden rule of cooking": never share a recipe you wouldn't use yourself. It's an approach that works—*ten million times over!*

Table Of Contents

Foreword

Successful parties begin with detailed planning. Plan with lists and more lists. Decide what kind of party you'd like to have. After that, decide the date and time and whom to invite. A large gathering allows you to invite a more varied mix of people with a wide range of personalities and professions. When planning parties for a small number of guests be sure guests are compatible.

Plan according to budget, ability and time. Keep it simple. Simplicity often equates to elegance. Plan recipes that can be made ahead, including some foods that can be frozen. Have a list of things to do and when to do them. Make two grocery lists – one for the make aheads and non-perishables and one for the last minute fresh items.

It is handy to jot down names of guests in a notebook. You will save time planning future parties if you keep a list of food and drink quantities previously consumed. Keep a record of the menu served. After the party, add reminders to serve more of a "big hit" the next time you entertain. Keeping a list will also help you avoid serving the same menu to the same guests at a future date.

Make your table the center of attraction. Even if you don't have fancy dishes, you can make your table appealing. Flowers are always a nice touch. Choose linen colors to complement your china. A neat and orderly setting will make any table look inviting.

Plan to have a little free time the day of the party to relax. Do not sound apologetic for food or surroundings. Accept compliments graciously. You deserve them. Let's have a party!

Jean Paré

Potluck Party

Potluck is a casual way to entertain. It is well suited for a large gathering or a small group. The host provides the space and atmosphere but meal preparation is shared by all.

What kind of potluck — mystery or planned? Mystery works better for a large group. For a small number of people, a planned menu is the safer way to go. To ensure a balanced meal ask your guests what course they would like to bring, whether salad, potatoes, vegetable or dessert, and decide how many it should serve. If a large number of guests will be present, you can have several items of each course or perhaps you will have enough guests to go the mystery route — real potluck. Remind guests that items should be toteable. The hostess/host could supply the meat dish as well as dinner rolls, butter, coffee, tea, cream, sugar and condiments.

To prevent food spoilage, be sure to have room in the fridge to keep cold foods chilled and oven space to keep hot foods hot. A temperature of 175°F to 200° F (80°C to 95°C) will suffice.

There will be a number of people in your kitchen putting the finishing touches to their dishes. Create a pleasant atmosphere by placing scented potpourri in a warming dish.

Table Decoration: Keep it small and simple since you don't know the sizes of containers people will be bringing. A small lighted candle or floral arrangement works well.

Theme And Occasion: Although there needn't be a theme, it is fun and interesting to choose one. Try an international theme highlighting a country, or celebrate the various holiday times of the year with colorful decorations and related food dishes. Natural "potluck" occasions could be for a surprise, a birthday or an office promotion.

Decoration: If you choose an international theme, ask your travel agent for some travel brochures. Hang up a map as well as some ornaments. Fill a large bowl with fruit that is characteristic of the chosen country. If having a birthday, surprise, or office party, balloons and streamers give a festive look.

Table Setting: If you know ahead what type of dish each guest is bringing, you can set the table accordingly. If not, set a knife, fork and teaspoon at each place. Add other serving or eating utensils as required once the dishes arrive. For a large number of guests you should consider serving buffet style.

Two Weeks Prior: Decide when to have your party and what theme you plan to have. Invite guests. Decide what each will bring and how many it should serve. As hostess/host, you should plan to supply the main course.

One Week Prior: Check your supply of coffee and other hot or cold drinks. Don't forget to ensure you have lots of ice. Go over your own food course to see if your grocery shopping list is complete. Order flowers.

One Day Prior: Set table if it isn't in use. Make your food dish if it can be prepared ahead.

Day Of Party: Buy cream and dinner rolls. Pick up flowers. One or two fresh cut flowers with a bit of greenery does wonders for the appearance of the bathroom. Set out fresh towels in the bathroom and check tissue. Cut and butter dinner rolls. Finish main dish, if necessary. Set out coffee pot or urn along with cups, saucers, cream pitcher and sugar bowl on the side table. Clean kitchen in preparation for guests' dishes.

Vegetable Mixture
One of the best combinations.

250 mL	1 cup	Sliced onion in rings, then quartered	Cook onion in boiling water for about 4 minutes until half done.
250 mL	1 cup	Boiling water	
2 × 284 mL	2 × 10 oz.	Frozen cauliflower	Add cauliflower and peas. Stir. Bring to a boil. Cook about 7 to 9 minutes until tender. Drain.
1 × 284 mL	1 × 10 oz.	Frozen peas	
30 mL	2 tbsp.	Chopped pimiento	Add pimiento, butter, basil, salt and pepper. Toss. Serves 8.
30 mL	2 tbsp.	Butter or margarine	
2 mL	½ tsp.	Basil	
2 mL	½ tsp.	Salt	
		Pepper, good sprinkle	**Pictured below.**

Bowl Courtesy Of:
Woodward's China Department

Shrimp Mousse *A real party attraction.*

2 x 7 g	2 x ¼ oz.	Unflavored gelatin	Sprinkle gelatin over water in small saucepan. Let stand 1 minute. Heat and stir until dissolved. Remove from heat.
125 mL	½ cup	Water	
250 g	8 oz.	Cream cheese, softened	Beat cream cheese with tomato soup in small mixing bowl until smooth. Beat in salad dressing, lemon juice, salt, onion powder and Worcestershire sauce. Add gelation mixture. Mix.
284 mL	10 oz.	Condensed tomato soup	
125 mL	½ cup	Salad dressing (or mayonnaise)	
30 mL	2 tbsp.	Lemon juice	
2 mL	½ tsp.	Salt	
2 mL	½ tsp.	Onion powder	
1 mL	¼ tsp.	Worcestershire sauce	
250 mL	1 cup	Finely chopped celery	Fold in remaining ingredients. Turn into 6 cup (1.35 mL) mold. Chill. Serve with toast cups or crackers. Decorate with Tomato Rose, page 11.
75 mL	⅓ cup	Finely chopped green pepper	
2 x 113 g	2 x 4 oz.	Canned small (or broken) shrimp, rinsed, drained and chopped	

Pictured on front cover.

Cheesy Rice
This bakes in the oven. Rice may be cooked ahead. Yummy.

500 mL	**2 cups**	Long grain rice	Cook rice in water for
1 L	**4 cups**	Water	15 minutes until tender and water is absorbed.
250 mL	**1 cup**	Sour cream	Add remaining ingredients. Stir.
500 mL	**2 cups**	Grated Monterey Jack cheese	Turn into 2 quart (2 L) casserole. Bake, uncovered, in 350°F
5 mL	**1 tsp.**	Salt	(175°C) oven for 30 to 35 min-
1 mL	**¼ tsp.**	Pepper	utes until hot. Serves 8.

Tomato Rose

Using a sharp paring knife begin at top, blossom end of tomato. Remove peel in 1 continuous strip, about ¾ inch (2 cm) wide. Wind the peel as for jelly roll, rolling center tighter than rest. Allow successive turns to fan out more. If necessary, secure with toothpick. Add mint leaves or parsley for a finishing touch.

Pictured on front cover.

Marble Cheesecake

This is better when made one day or even two days ahead. Serve at room temperature.

Crust

100 mL	6 tbsp.	Butter or margarine
350 mL	1½ cups	Graham cracker crumbs
30 mL	2 tbsp.	Granulated sugar
30 mL	2 tbsp.	Cocoa

Melt butter in saucepan. Stir in graham crumbs, sugar and cocoa. Pack into bottom of ungreased 9 inch (22 cm) springform pan. Bake in 350°F (175°C) oven for 10 minutes.

Filling

3 x 250 g	3 x 8 oz.	Cream cheese, softened
250 mL	1 cup	Granulated sugar
50 mL	3 tbsp.	All-purpose flour

Beat cream cheese, sugar and flour in mixing bowl until smooth.

4	4	Large eggs
7 mL	1½ tsp.	Vanilla
250 mL	1 cup	Whipping cream

Beat in eggs slowly, 1 at a time. Add vanilla and whipping cream. Mix. Measure out 1½ cups (350 mL) and reserve. Pour remaining batter over crust.

2 x 28 g	2 x 1 oz.	Unsweetened chocolate baking squares
350 mL	1½ cups	Reserved cheese mixture

Place chocolate squares in saucepan. Heat over low heat, stirring often, until melted. Cool. Stir into reserved batter. Spoon dabs over top of batter in pan. Using a knife, cut zig zag through batter. Bake in 350°F (175°C) oven for 1 hour until a knife inserted off center comes out clean.

Pictured on front cover.

Tossed Salad

Toss contents of the two bowls together when ready to serve.

Dressing

125 mL	½ cup	Salad dressing (or mayonnaise)	Stir all 6 ingredients together in small bowl. Chill.
60 mL	¼ cup	Milk	
2 mL	½ tsp.	Prepared mustard	
5 mL	1 tsp.	Granulated sugar	
0.5 mL	⅛ tsp.	Garlic powder	
0.5 mL	⅛ tsp.	Onion powder	

Salad

2 L	9 cups	Assorted greens, torn or cut, lightly packed	Tear greens into large bowl. Add almonds. Chill. Just before serving add dressing and toss. Serves 8 to 10.
60 mL	¼ cup	Toasted sliced almonds	

Pictured on back cover.

Cheesecake

When beating eggs into a cheesecake, beat only until blended. Do not over beat. While cooling, the sides and center shrink down. Running a knife around the sides of pan as soon as you remove cake from oven, will yield a more even look.

Time Saver

If serving large amounts of salad, you will find it is much faster to cut greens rather than to tear them. They will last at least a whole day before edges begin to brown.

Heavenly Hash

A great make-ahead to get a potluck off to a good start.

250 mL	1 cup	Chopped onion	Sauté onion and bacon in
3	3	Bacon slices, diced	frying pan until onion is soft.
900 g	2 lbs.	Lean ground beef	Add ground beef. Scramble-fry until browned.
125 mL	½ cup	Grated medium Cheddar cheese	Stir in cheese and celery. Simmer slowly for 30 minutes.
450 mL	2 cups	Chopped celery	
700 mL	3 cups	Macaroni	Cook macaroni in boiling water, cooking oil and salt in large uncovered Dutch oven 5 to 7 minutes until tender but firm. Drain. Return macaroni to pot. Add meat mixture.
4 L	4 qts.	Boiling water	
15 mL	1 tbsp.	Cooking oil	
15 mL	1 tbsp.	Salt	
2 x 284 mL	2 x 10 oz.	Condensed cream of mushroom soup	Add soups. Stir. Turn into 3 quart (3 L) casserole. Bake, uncovered, in 350°F (175°C) oven for 35 minutes until hot. Serves 8 to 10.
2 x 284 mL	2 x 10 oz.	Condensed tomato soup	

Mellow Meaty Casserole *A make-ahead potluck pleaser.*

680 g	1½ lbs.	Lean ground beef	Scramble-fry ground beef
250 mL	1 cup	Chopped onion	and onion in margarine until
30 mL	2 tbsp.	Margarine (butter browns too fast)	browned.
2 × 213 mL	2 × 7½ oz.	Tomato sauce	Stir in tomato sauce.
250 g	8 oz.	Fettuccine	Cook fettuccine in large
2.5 L	2½ qts.	Boiling water	uncovered saucepan in
15 mL	1 tbsp.	Cooking oil	boiling water, cooking oil
10 mL	2 tsp.	Salt	and salt until tender but firm, about 5 to 7 minutes. Drain.
250 g	8 oz.	Cream cheese, softened	Stir first 2 cheeses and sour
250 mL	1 cup	Cottage cheese	cream together. Spread half
125 mL	½ cup	Sour cream	of noodles in 3 quart (3 L) casserole. Spoon cheese mixture over top. Cover with remaining noodles. Pour meat mixture over all. May be chilled at this point until later. Bake, uncovered, in 350°F (175°C) oven for about 35 minutes until bubbly hot.
250 mL	1 cup	Grated medium Cheddar cheese	Sprinkle with Cheddar cheese. Bake 5 to 10 minutes more until cheese melts. Serves 8.

Citrus Ice Ring *Make days ahead.*

3	3	Lemons
1	1	Lime
6	6	Maraschino cherries, drained well
		Water

Have lemons and limes the same size if possible. Cut in half lengthwise. With cut side down, cut into ¼ inch (6 mm) slices. A ring mold with grooves in the bottom is ideal for this mold. With rind edge down, stand slices up around circle. Place 1 lime, 2 lemon, 1 cherry, 2 lemon close together. Repeat 5 more times. Pour in enough water to be ½ inch deep. Freeze. Pour in 1 inch (2.5 cm) more water. Freeze. Repeat until mold is full. Run cold water over bottom to unmold. Place round side up in punch.

Pictured on front cover.

Party Flower Napkins

1. Fold square napkin in half to form triangle.

2. Fold up bottom to make a 3 inch (7.5 cm) cuff.

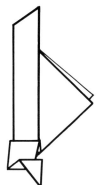

3. Turn sideways. Using your fingers, make about 1 inch (2.5 cm) pleats along cuff.

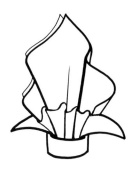

4 Hold pleats firmly. Insert bottom pleated cuff into napkin ring. Stand upright. Arrange it so it flairs out evenly.

Pictured on back cover.

Punch Sparkler *A golden refreshing drink.*

700 mL	3 cups	Pineapple juice	Pour juices and water into
170 g	6 oz.	Frozen concentrated	punch bowl. Stir. Chill until
		orange juice	just before serving.
170g	6 oz.	Frozen concentrated	
		lemonade	
350 mL	1½ cups	Grapefruit juice	
1 L	4½ cups	Water	
700 mL	3 cups	Ginger ale	Add ginger ale. Stir gently.
		Citrus Ice Ring, see page 16	Place ice ring in center. Makes 108 oz. (3 L)

Pictured on front cover.

1. Super Salad page 26
2. Mock Pink Champagne page 32
3. Stuffed Steak Supreme page 27
4. Sprouts And Carrots page 30
5. Special Rice page 28

China And Silverware Courtesy Of:
Reed's China And Gift Shop

Dinner Party

Number Of Guests: A dinner party can be for as many guests as you can seat comfortably at your dining room table. You will also need to consider how many place settings and serving dishes you have. For most, eight to ten people is a good number.

Menu: Include some food items not considered every day fare or serve a favorite dish you're known for. It is best to plan your menu to include a variety of complementary colors, textures and flavors. For example, if you plan a seafood cocktail, do not serve fish as a main course.

Seating Arrangement: It is your party, so you can seat people where you like. A more formal custom is to seat a gentleman guest of honor to the right of the hostess and a lady guest of honor to the right of the host. Place cards are a great convenience. Set them above the plate.

Table Setting: A white table cloth over a silence cloth is always a good choice. Again, work with what you have. Flowers should be low enough so guests don't have to look around or through them. Candles shouldn't be so thick as to have to peek around them.

Place Setting: Diagrams of some of the more popular table settings follow.

Plates and cutlery should be 1 inch (2.5 cm) in from edge of table. Set forks to the left in order of use, beginning from the outside. The exception is the seafood cocktail fork which can be placed to the right of the knives and spoons or may be placed on the plate with the cocktail. Knives go the right of the dinner plate in order of use from the outside in. Remember, the rounded cutting edge always faces the plate. If salad requires cutting before eating, set a salad knife to the right of the dinner knife. If salad is served after the main course set salad cutlery to the inside of dinner cutlery. Spoons go to the right of the knives, also in order of use from the outside in. The bread and butter plate is placed to the left of the dinner plate above the tip of the dinner (largest) fork. It can also be placed to the left of the forks to give more room for food on the table. The butter knife is placed on the bread and butter plate parallel to the table edge. The rounded edge faces down toward the edge of the table. Allow as much room as reasonably possible between place settings.

Too much cutlery on a table can be overwhelming. A thoughtful hostess/host never makes guests feel uncomfortable. Set only the silver needed. If more is required, it can be brought in with each course. Occasionally the cutlery for dessert/coffee is placed above the dinner plate. Be sure all dishes and cutlery are evenly placed and your table will look organized.

Water goblets go above the tip of the dinner (largest) knife. Wine glasses are positioned to the right and slightly down from the water goblet.

The placement of napkins is flexible. They are often positioned to the left of the fork with the open corners closest to the bottom of the forks. They may also be placed on the bread and butter or dinner plate, in water goblets or in wine glasses.

Serving: The most convenient way to serve is family style. Bowls of food are placed on the dinner table for guests to help themselves, then passed to the left. Place serving utensils beside the dishes, not in them. People take as much or as little as they want. Another option is to serve the plates in the kitchen and bring them to the table. Plates are usually served from the left and removed from the right. Wine is always served from the right unless it is passed for guests to help themselves. Coffee and tea are also served from the right. A third serving option is to have the host carve and serve the meat and the hostess serve the vegetables at the table.

To signify you are finished, place your knife and fork in the four o'clock position on your dinner plate. The rounded cutting edge of the knife should be to the right of, and facing, the fork.

Water And Wine: Place iced water and wine on the table before seating guests. A pitcher of milk is common as well.

Dinner Music: Keep it low enough so as not to inhibit conversation.

Table Clearing: Never stack dishes at the table. Carry to the kitchen. Clear food service dishes as well as salt and pepper before serving dessert and coffee.

Dessert: If only dessert is on the table and no cutlery, a dessert fork or spoon may be placed to the right of the dessert plate.

Coffee/Tea: At one time, a small spoon was placed on the saucer behind the cup for stirring cream and sugar. It is now common practice to place a few spoons on a tray with the cream and sugar.

Meal's End: If leaving the table during the meal, place your napkin on the seat of your chair. At the end of the meal, do not fold your napkin, but gather it and place it on the table to the left of your place setting.

Two Weeks Prior: Send or phone invitations. Indicate time, date and dress requirements. Ask for RSVP's.

One Week Prior: Polish silver. Make ice and bag it. Check supply of refreshments. Order flowers. Avoid strongly scented flowers for the table. A few scented ones would be nice for the bathroom.

Two To Three Days Prior: Determine final seating arrangement based on RSVP's received, and write place cards.

Day of Party: Buy fresh bread/dinner rolls and cream. Pick up flowers. Buy fresh produce. Chill white wine. Empty kitchen and bathroom garbage containers. Empty dishwasher. Place fresh towels in the bathroom. Check tissues. Clear out newspapers and magazines.

One Hour Before: Open red wine. Get dressed and get set to party!

Basic Setting

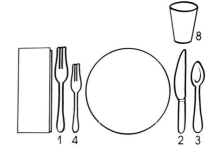

1. Dinner Fork
2. Dinner Knife
3. Teaspoon
4. Dessert Fork
5. Salad Fork
6. Soup Spoon
7. Juice Glass
8. Water Glass
9. Wine Glass
10. Butter Knife

Setting for main course and dessert. This works if salad is served along with the main course.

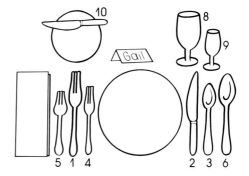

Setting for salad course and main course. Teaspoon can be used for a spoon-eaten dessert or dessert forks can be brought in on dessert plates.

Setting for soup, salad, main course and dessert. To serve salad after the main course, move salad fork to the right of dinner fork.

Seafood Squares

These can be made ahead. Cover to reheat.

500 mL	2 cups	Tea biscuit mix	Stir biscuit mix, milk and onion powder together in bowl to form a soft ball. Press onto bottom of 9 x 13 inch (22 x 33 cm) pan. Bake in 375°F (190°C) oven for 15 minutes to partially cook.
125 mL	½ cup	Milk	
1 mL	¼ tsp.	Onion powder	
250 mL	1 cup	Grated medium or sharp Cheddar cheese	Sprinkle crust with both cheeses, shrimp and crabmeat.
250 mL	1 cup	Grated Monterey Jack cheese	
2 x 113 g	2 x 4 oz.	Canned broken shrimp, rinsed and drained	
1 x 142 g	1 x 5 oz.	Canned crabmeat, drained, cartilage removed,	
6	6	Large eggs	Beat eggs until frothy. Add cream, salt and pepper. Mix. Pour over top of crabmeat. Return to oven and bake about 35 minutes until an inserted knife comes out clean. Let stand 5 to 10 minutes. Cut into squares. Serve warm. Garnish with sprigs of dill and cherry tomato wedges. Makes 54 squares.
450 mL	2 cups	Light cream (half and half)	
2 mL	½ tsp.	Salt	
1 mL	¼ tsp.	Pepper	

Pictured on page 25.

Dinner Rolls *So easy.*

175 mL	¾ cup	Milk	Heat milk in small saucepan until it reaches the boiling point. Pour into mixing bowl.
50 mL	3 tbsp.	Butter or margarine	Stir in butter to melt. Add salt and cold water. Cool until lukewarm.
7 mL	1½ tsp.	Salt	
175 mL	¾ cup	Cold water	
450 mL	2 cups	All-purpose flour	Add first amount of flour and yeast. Beat until smooth.
15 mL	1 tbsp.	Instant yeast	
350 mL	1½ cups	All-purpose flour	Stir in remaining flour. If dough is too sticky, stir in a bit more flour. Mix. Knead on lightly floured surface for about 5 minutes. Place in greased bowl, turning so top surface is greased also. Cover. Let rise in warm place until double in size, about 1½ hours. Shape into balls. Arrange on greased baking sheet. Let rise to double in size, about 1 hour. Bake in 375°F (190°C) oven for about 25 minutes. Makes 2 dozen.

Seafood
Squares

Super Salad

Chill dressing and salad separately. Combine when ready to serve.

Super Dressing

30 mL	2 tbsp.	Cooking oil	Measure all 7 ingredients
30 mL	2 tbsp.	Red wine vinegar	into jar. Put on lid. Shake
5 mL	1 tsp.	Dijon mustard	well. Chill.
2 mL	½ tsp.	Dill weed	
0.5 mL	⅛ tsp.	Garlic powder (or ½ tsp. 2 mL, fresh minced)	
2 mL	½ tsp.	Salt	
2 mL	½ tsp.	Pepper	

Salad

1 L	4 cups	Broccoli florets	Cook broccoli in small
125 mL	½ cup	Water	amount of water until tender-crisp. Drain. Cool.
500 mL	2 cups	Thinly sliced fresh mushrooms	Combine cooked broccoli with mushrooms, pea pods
170 g	7 oz.	Frozen pea pods, thawed and drained	and almonds in large bowl. Chill.
125 mL	½ cup	Toasted slivered or sliced almonds	
1	1	Head of Romaine lettuce, torn	When ready to serve divide lettuce among 8 salad plates.
125 mL	½ cup	Light cream (half and half) Prepared Super Dressing	Add light cream to dressing in jar. Shake. Pour over vegetables in bowl. Toss. Spoon over lettuce. Serves 8.

Pictured on page 19.

Stuffed Steak Supreme

Prepare early in the day to be cooked later.

1.13 kg	2½ lbs.	Round steak, thin enough to roll	Spread steak with mustard.
15 mL	1 tbsp.	Dijon mustard	
175 mL	¾ cup	Chopped onion	Sauté onion and carrot in butter in frying pan until soft. Remove from heat.
175 mL	¾ cup	Grated carrot	
25 mL	1½ tbsp.	Butter or margarine	
250 mL	1 cup	Kernel corn	Mix in next 7 ingredients. Spoon evenly over steak. Roll up as for jelly roll. Tie with string.
175 mL	¾ cup	Dry bread crumbs	
15 mL	1 tbsp.	Soy sauce	
50 mL	3 tbsp.	Grated Parmesan cheese	
1 mL	¼ tsp.	Garlic powder	
4 mL	¾ tsp.	Salt	
1 mL	¼ tsp.	Pepper	
15 mL	1 tbsp.	Cooking oil	Place steak rolls in small roaster. Brush tops and sides with cooking oil.
5 mL	1 tsp.	Beef bouillon powder	Stir bouillon powder into hot water. Pour around meat. Cover. Cook in 325°F (160°C) oven until tender, about 1½ hours. Remove string. Serve in slices on serving platter. Serves 8.
125 mL	½ cup	Hot water	

Pictured on page 19.

Special Rice
Make this ahead if you like. Stir-fry to reheat.

2 x 180 g	2 x 6 oz.	Packages long grain and wild rice
1 L	4½ cups	Water
2	2	Seasoning packets

Combine first 3 ingredients in saucepan. Bring to a boil. Simmer, covered, until rice is tender and moisture has been absorbed, about 15 to 20 minutes.

284 mL	10 oz.	Canned mushroom pieces, drained
30 mL	2 tbsp.	Butter or margarine
30 mL	2 tbsp.	Toasted slivered almonds

Stir in mushroom pieces, butter and almonds. Makes 6⅔ cups (1.5 L) Serves 8 to 10.

Pictured on page 19.

Baked Alaskas page 29

Plate Courtesy Of:
Reed's China And Gift Shop

Baked Alaskas
With these in the freezer it takes no time to brown and serve.

1	1	Jelly roll, white or chocolate, 3-3½ inches (7.5-9 cm) in diameter	Cut 8 slices at least ½ inch (12 mm) thick. Place on baking tray.
5	5	Egg whites (large), room temperature	Beat egg whites, vanilla and salt in mixing bowl until soft peaks form.
5 mL	1 tsp.	Vanilla	
1 mL	¼ tsp.	Salt	
175 mL	¾ cup	Granulated sugar	Gradually add sugar while beating until stiff and sugar is dissolved.
8	8	Ice cream scoops, your choice of flavor	Place scoop of ice cream on each slice of jelly roll. Quickly cover each completely with ⅛ meringue. Place in freezer. When ready to serve, bake in center part of 450°F (230°C) oven until golden, about 2 minutes. Serve immediately. Serves 8.

Pictured on page 28.

Sprouts And Carrots

Make carrot mixture ahead. Heat and add to hot sprouts when ready to serve.

Metric	Imperial	Ingredient	Instructions
60 mL	¼ cup	Butter or margarine	Melt butter in large saucepan. Add carrot and onion. Sauté until soft. Do not brown.
350 mL	1½ cups	Grated carrot	
125 mL	½ cup	Finely chopped onion	
10 mL	2 tsp.	All-purpose flour	Mix in flour, bouillon powder, mustard, salt and pepper. Stir in milk until it boils and thickens. Keep warm while Brussels sprouts cook.
2 mL	½ tsp.	Chicken bouillon powder	
5 mL	1 tsp.	Prepared mustard	
2 mL	½ tsp.	Salt	
0.5 mL	⅛ tsp.	Pepper	
125 mL	½ cup	Milk	
3 x 284 g	3 x 10 oz.	Frozen Brussels sprouts	Cook Brussels sprouts in water until barely tender. Drain. Add carrot mixture. Toss. Serves 8.
		Water	

Pictured on page 19.

Dinner Party

There is no better way to relax and enjoy good food and surroundings than with friends. Friends can be new or long term. When meeting new people, a dinner party is a great way to get to know them. When people dine together, self consciousness disappears and conversation fills the air.

Lily Napkins

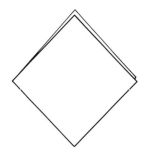

1. Fold napkin into quarters with open corners to the top.

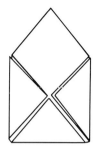

2. Fold side corners in to meet in center. Fold bottom corner up to meet in center. Turn over carefully.

3. Gather into narrow pleats at bottom.

4. Place in napkin ring. Lay flat. Arrange top of napkin to resemble a lily.

Mock Pink Champagne

Have most of this assembled. Add ginger ale and serve.

250 mL	1 cup	Water	Combine water and sugar in small saucepan. Heat and stir to dissolve sugar.
250 mL	1 cup	Granulated sugar	
170 g	6 oz.	Frozen concentrated lemonade	Combine lemonade, orange juice and grenadine in punch bowl. Add water-sugar mixture. Chill.
170 g	6 oz.	Frozen concentrated orange juice	
50 mL	¼ cup	Grenadine	
2 L	9 cups	Ginger ale, chilled Ice cubes (optional)	Just before serving add ginger ale. Pour over ice in glasses. Garnish with fresh strawberries. Makes 12 cups (2.7 L).

Pictured below.
Also pictured on page 19.

Chilled Berry Dessert

Good flavor, good color, good looks.

Crust

250 mL	1 cup	Butter or margarine	Melt butter in saucepan. Stir in flour and sugar. Pack into 9 x 13 inch (22 x 33 cm) pan. Bake in 350°F (175°C) oven for about 15 minutes until browned. Cool.
500 mL	2 cups	All-purpose flour	
125 mL	½ cup	Brown sugar, packed	

Filling

1 x 7 g	1 x ¼ oz.	Unflavored gelatin	Stir first 2 ingredients well in bowl. Add boiling water, stirring until dissolved.
2 x 85 g	2 x 3 oz.	Strawberry flavored gelatin (jelly powder)	
450 mL	2 cups	Boiling water	
125 mL	½ cup	Sour cream	Whisk in sour cream and salad dressing. Add ice cream and raspberries. Stir until melted and beginning to set. Pour over crust. Chill.
50 mL	¼ cup	Salad dressing (or mayonnaise)	
500 mL	2 cups	Strawberry ice cream	
425 g	15 oz.	Frozen sliced raspberries in syrup	
500 mL	2 cups	Frozen whipped topping, thawed	Serve with a dollop of whipped topping and a sprinkle of grated chocolate. Makes 15 to 18 servings.
		Grated chocolate	

Duchess Potatoes

Brown these at the last moment.

1.14 kg	2½ lbs.	Potatoes, peeled and cut up	Cook potatoes in water until tender. Drain. Return to heat, shaking pot to keep from burning, until dry. Put potatoes through ricer or mash very well.
		Water	
100 mL	6 tbsp.	Butter or margarine	Add next 6 ingredients. Mash well. Shape into mounds with fingers or use a large star pipe. Place on greased pan.
50 mL	3 tbsp.	Milk	
4 mL	¾ tsp.	Salt	
		Pepper, sprinkle	
2	2	Large eggs, beaten	
15 mL	1 tbsp.	All-purpose flour	
1	1	Large egg, beaten	Brush carefully with beaten egg. Bake in 400°F (205°C) oven for 5 to 7 minutes until golden brown. Garnish with fresh parsley. Makes 20.

Pictured on this page.

Platter Courtesy Of:
The Bay Housewares Department

Baked Tomatoes

Assemble this dish early in the day and bake when ready.

50 mL	3 tbsp.	Butter or margarine	Melt butter in frying pan.
150 mL	⅔ cup	Chopped onion	Add next 5 ingredients.
2 mL	½ tsp.	Salt	Sauté until onion is soft.
		Pepper, sprinkle	
5 mL	1 tsp.	Parsley flakes	
2 mL	½ tsp.	Basil	
5	5	Medium tomatoes, sliced ¼ inch (6 mm) thick	Overlap tomato slices in bottom of 9 x 13 inch (22 x 33 cm) pan. Spoon onion mixture over top being sure to get some on each piece. Cook now or cover and chill until needed. Remove cover. Bake in 350°F (175°C) oven until hot and bubbly, about 20 to 25 minutes. Serves 6 to 8.

Pictured on this page.

Dish Courtesy Of:
Ikea

Crusty Chicken

Most attractive and tasty. Good dinner dish.

125 mL	½ cup	Butter or margarine	Melt butter in saucepan. Stir
125 mL	½ cup	Salad dressing (or	in salad dressing and
		mayonnaise)	mustard.
15 mL	1 tbsp.	Prepared mustard	
450 mL	2 cups	Fine dry bread crumbs	Mix next 6 ingredients in shallow bowl.
5 mL	1 tsp.	Parsley flakes	
4 mL	¾ tsp.	Poultry seasoning	
2 mL	½ tsp.	Onion powder	
5 mL	1 tsp.	Salt	
1 mL	¼ tsp.	Pepper	
6-7	6-7	Chicken breasts, halved, skin and bone removed	Flatten chicken breasts to an even thickness. Dip into butter mixture. Coat with crumbs. Arrange on greased baking pan. Bake in 350°F (175°C) oven for 45 minutes until tender. Makes 12 to 14 half breast servings.

Gherkin Salad *A fabulous pickle salad.*

1 x 85 g	1 x 3 oz.	Lime flavored gelatin (jelly powder)	Dissolve gelatin in water in bowl.
250 mL	1 cup	Boiling water	
398 mL	14 oz.	Crushed pineapple with juice	Add pineapple with juice and lemon juice. Stir. Chill, stirring and scraping down sides often, until it starts to thicken.
30 mL	2 tbsp.	Lemon juice	
125 mL	½ cup	Chopped gherkins	Add next 5 ingredients. Stir. Spoon into 8 individual salad molds or 4 cup (1 L) mold. Chill.
125 mL	½ cup	Grated cabbage	
75 mL	⅓ cup	Grated carrot	
30 mL	2 tbsp.	Chopped pimiento	
1 mL	¼ tsp.	Salt	
8	8	Lettuce leaves	Unmold individual salads onto lettuce. Top each with ½ tsp. (2 mL) dollop salad dressing. Makes eight, ½ cup (125 mL) servings.
20 mL	4 tsp.	Salad dressing (or mayonnaise)	

Peach Chutney

Have chilled and ready to serve with meat.

250 mL	1 cup	Peach jam
125 mL	½ cup	Light colored raisins
60 mL	¼ cup	Chopped walnuts
60 mL	¼ cup	Cider vinegar
2 mL	½ tsp.	Grated orange peel
1 mL	¼ tsp.	Ginger
0.5 mL	⅛ tsp.	Onion powder

Combine all ingredients in saucepan. Stir. Simmer slowly, stirring often until it thickens. Place a small spoonful on cold saucer. It should be the thickness of a soft jam. Time will be about 20 minutes. Makes a generous 1 cup (250 mL).

Cranberry Orange Punch

Good color. Partly a make-ahead.

1.13 L	40 oz.	Bottled cranberry cocktail
190 g	6 oz.	Frozen concentrated orange juice
2 L	8 cups	Ginger ale

Combine cranberry and orange juice. Add ginger ale shortly before serving.

	Ice cubes
	Orange slices

Pour over ice cubes in glasses. Garnish with orange slices. Makes 14 cups (3.15 L).

1. **Apricot Daiquiris page 46**
2. **Strawberry Slush page 42**
3. **Cross Bones page 49**
4. **Porky Pops page 51**
5. **Choco Peanut Squares page 47**
6. **Chip Dip page 49**

Dishes And Glassware Courtesy Of:
Le Gnome

China Bowl Courtesy Of:
Reed's China And Gift Shop

Kids' Party

Guests: Keep to numbers that can easily be managed. This is especially true where young children are concerned. A good rule of thumb is to invite one child per year. Six years old would mean six guests. Be sure you can seat everyone at the table. It is much safer to serve food that way. Keep in mind that their attention span is short, their energy level high and their appetites small. State beginning and ending times on the invitations. Quite a short party, perhaps two hours, is usually plenty for young children.

Menu Planning: Depending on age, let the youngsters help in planning. Keep in mind the young get too exited to eat much food while older teens have very hearty appetites. Finger foods or fork foods are best for all ages. Check for any allergies of the guests, especially milk or dairy products, nuts and apple juice.

Activities: For preteen and early teenage youngsters, it is best to have table seating room. While their attention span is longer than the younger ones, they do like to keep moving. Have games planned outdoors if weather permits. They can suggest and help plan games of all kinds.

You will probably require some input to host a teen party. Perhaps a certain kind of music will be high on the list. Kids of any age will enjoy helping in the planning of activities.

Decorations: Develop a theme, from whatever animal is in style at the moment to some far off alien world. Follow through with some decorating. Nothing is easier or more economical than brightly colored balloons. Streamers add a festive touch. No actual theme is needed with balloons and streamers. The mood is set.

Table Settings: Try to carry matching colors throughout. A brightly colored bed sheet makes an excellent tablecloth. Small favors can be set at each plate. Draw silly faces on napkins, or try to 'match' your guests facial features (eg. glasses, freckles, missing tooth). A themed paper tablecloth is handy as are plastic placemats.

Invitations: Decorate the invitations according to the theme. Draw or paste on pictures cut from magazines or catalogs. Photocopy or use a computer to design the entire invitation. Use bright colors. Hand deliver the invitations for young children directly to their parents.

Two Weeks Prior: Decide theme of party, the date and time, number of guests and activities. Distribute invitations.

One Week Prior: If having a cake, bake and freeze it or place a special order for one. Plan the menu. Do the freeze-aheads.

One Day Prior: Assemble all game-related items. If giving prizes, wrap in cheery paper. Remove food from freezer to refrigerator. Decorate cake. Pick up groceries.

Day of Party: Pick up cake, if ordered. Decorate party room. Finish preparing all food and refreshments.

Mashed Potatoes *Actually a puffed potato casserole.*

1.6 kg	3½ lbs.	Potatoes, peeled and cut Water	Cook potatoes in water until tender. Drain. Mash.
250 g	8 oz.	Cream cheese, softened	Beat cream cheese, egg, salt, onion powder and pepper in small mixing bowl until smooth. Add to potatoes. Mash. Turn into greased 3 quart (3 L) casserole.
1	1	Large egg	
5 mL	1 tsp.	Salt	
2 mL	½ tsp.	Onion powder	
0.5 mL	⅛ tsp.	Pepper	
		Paprika, sprinkle	Sprinkle with paprika. Bake, uncovered, in 350°F (175°C) oven for 45 minutes. Serves 8.

Strawberry Slush *Make just before serving.*

170 g	6 oz.	Concentrated frozen lemonade	Combine all ingredients in blender. Blend until smooth and icy. Pour into glasses. Serve with wide straws or spoons. Makes a scant 3 cups (675 mL).
½ x 600 g	½ x 21 oz.	Frozen whole strawberries	
175 mL	¾ cup	Water	

Pictured on page 39.

STRAWBERRY DAIQUIRIS: Use fresh strawberries rather than frozen. Add 1 cup (250 mL) crushed ice. Blend.

Monkey Bread

Baked and served in a clump. Kids pull off their own portion.

3	3	Tubes of refrigerator biscuits (10 to a can)	Separate biscuits. Cut each biscuit into 4 pieces.
250 mL	1 cup	Granulated sugar	Mix sugar and cinnamon in bag. Shake to coat each biscuit piece. Pile evenly into greased and floured 12 cup (2.7 L) bundt pan.
5 mL	1 tsp.	Cinnamon	
125 mL	½ cup	Butter or margarine	Heat butter and brown sugar in saucepan to melt butter. Stir. Spoon over biscuits. Bake in 350°F (175°C) oven for about 20 minutes. Let stand for 10 minutes. Unmold onto plate. Cover to store or to freeze. Pull apart to eat. Serves 8.
250 mL	1 cup	Brown sugar, packed	

Pictured on this page.

Tray Courtesy Of:
Ikea

Always On A Sundae *A mouth watering freezer asset.*

125 mL	½ cup	Butter or margarine
600 mL	2⅔ cups	Vanilla wafer crumbs
150 mL	⅔ cup	Finely chopped walnuts

Melt butter in saucepan. Stir in crumbs and walnuts. Divide in half. Press one half into 8 inch (20 cm) springform pan. Reserve second half for layers. Bake in 350°F (175°C) oven for 8 to 10 minutes until browned. Cool.

500 mL	2 cups	Vanilla ice cream, softened
		Reserved crumbs
125 mL	½ cup	Butterscotch sundae topping

Spread vanilla ice cream over cooled crust. Sprinkle with ⅓ reserved crumbs. Drizzle with butterscotch topping. Freeze.

500 mL	2 cups	Strawberry ice cream, softened
		Reserved crumbs
125 mL	½ cup	Strawberry sundae topping (or jam)

Repeat with strawberry layer. Freeze.

Continued on next page.

125 mL	½ cup	Chocolate ice cream, softened
125 mL	½ cup	Reserved crumbs Chocolate sundae topping
500 mL	2 cups	Frozen whipped topping, thawed

Pictured below.

Repeat with chocolate layer keeping in mind it's the top decorative layer. Freeze.

To serve, spread with whipped topping or place dollop on side when serving. Remove sides of pan. Cut with sharp knife dipped in hot water. Serves 8 to 12.

Plate Courtesy Of:
The Bay China Department

Snap Peas And Carrots *Colorful and sauced lightly.*

500 mL	2 cups	Thinly sliced carrots	Cook carrots in water until
250 mL	1 cup	Water	tender-crisp.
2 × 170 g	2 × 6 oz.	Frozen pea pods	Add pea pods. Stir. Bring to a boil. Cook for 3 to 5 minutes until tender-crisp. Drain.
10 mL	2 tsp.	Water	In small saucepan stir water
5 mL	1 tsp.	Cornstarch	and cornstarch together.
15 mL	1 tbsp.	Soy sauce	Add soy sauce, onion salt
1 mL	¼ tsp.	Onion salt	and butter. Heat and stir
30 mL	2 tbsp.	Butter or margarine	until it boils and thickens. Stir into vegetables. Makes 8 servings.

Apricot Daiquiris *Prepare in a jiffy when needed. Use peaches for peach daiquiris.*

398 mL	14 oz.	Canned apricots with juice (or peaches)	Combine all ingredients in blender. Blend until smooth
450 mL	2 cups	Prepared orange juice	and icy. Makes 4½ cups (1 L).
60 mL	¼ cup	Frozen concentrated lemonade	
250 mL	1 cup	Crushed ice	**Pictured on page 39.**

Choco Peanut Squares

Make lots of these ahead. Delicious.

175 mL	¾ cup	Butter or margarine, softened	
60 mL	¼ cup	Smooth peanut butter	
225 mL	1 cup	Brown sugar, packed	
1	1	Large egg	
5 mL	1 tsp.	Vanilla	
450 mL	2 cups	All-purpose flour	

In mixing bowl cream butter, first amount of peanut butter and sugar. Mix in egg and vanilla. Stir in flour. Pat in greased 9 x 9 inch (22 x 22 cm) pan. Bake in 350°F (175°C) oven for 15 to 20 minutes until an inserted wooden pick comes out clean.

250 mL	1 cup	Semisweet chocolate chips
125 mL	½ cup	Smooth peanut butter

Melt chocolate chips and second amount of peanut butter in small saucepan. Spread over top. Cool. Cuts into 36 squares.

Pictured on page 39.

Ice Cream

Ice cream is always a suitable and welcome addition when serving squares. Choose the same or a different flavor from the squares.

To prevent the formation of ice crystals between "ice cream attacks", press plastic wrap over top, touching ice cream.

Toads

Serve hot from the oven or reheat later.

15 mL	1 tbsp.	Cooking oil	Heat first amount of cooking oil in frying pan. Add sausages and brown.
12	12	Cocktail size sausages (or small sausages, halved)	
225 mL	1 cup	All-purpose flour	Place flour, salt, egg and milk in small mixing bowl. Beat until smooth.
1 mL	¼ tsp.	Salt	
1	1	Large egg	
275 mL	1¼ cups	Milk	
30 mL	2 tbsp.	Cooking oil	Put ½ tsp. (2 mL) remaining cooking oil and 1 small browned sausage into each muffin cup. Heat in 425°F (220°C) oven for 5 minutes. Pour milk mixture quickly over each sausage. Bake for 20 minutes until golden brown and risen. Makes 12.

Pictured on this page.

Chip Dip
Make this the day you need it or make several days ahead.

250 mL	1 cup	Salad dressing (or mayonnaise)	Stir first 7 ingredients together in small bowl. Add a bit
5 mL	1 tsp.	Soy sauce	more milk if needed. Chill.
1 mL	¼ tsp.	Onion powder	Makes 1 cup (250 mL) dip.
2 mL	½ tsp.	Parsley flakes	
5 mL	1 tsp.	Red wine vinegar	
1 mL	¼ tsp.	Ginger	
30 mL	2 tbsp.	Milk	
		Potato chips	Serve with potato chips
		Assorted raw vegetables	and/or raw vegetables.

Pictured on page 39.

Cross Bones
Bones you can chew on.

15 mL	1 tbsp.	Paprika	Place first 9 ingredients in
10 mL	2 tsp.	Poultry seasoning	plastic or paper bag. Mix.
10 mL	2 tsp.	Parsley flakes	
2 mL	½ tsp.	Salt	
2 mL	½ tsp.	Celery salt	
2 mL	½ tsp.	Onion salt	
1 mL	¼ tsp.	Garlic powder	
1 mL	¼ tsp.	Pepper	
60 mL	¼ cup	Fine dry bread crumbs	
8	8	Chicken drumsticks	Add 2 drumsticks at a time. Shake to coat. Arrange on foil lined baking pan. Cook in 400°F (205°C) oven for 40 to 45 minutes until tender. Makes 8.

Pictured on page 39.

Sloppy Joes
Make ahead. Heat when needed. Freezes well.

30 mL	2 tbsp.	Butter or margarine	Melt butter in frying pan.
500 mL	2 cups	Chopped onion	Add onion and ground beef
1 kg	2 lbs.	Lean ground beef	½ at a time. Fry until browned. Turn into large Dutch oven.
125 mL	½ cup	Ketchup	Add next 8 ingredients. Stir.
30 mL	2 tbsp.	Vinegar	Bring to a boil, stirring often.
30 mL	2 tbsp.	Granulated sugar	Makes 5¼ cups (1.18 L).
15 mL	1 tbsp.	Prepared mustard	
7 mL	1½ tsp.	Salt	
2 mL	½ tsp.	Pepper	
10 mL	2 tsp.	Worcestershire sauce	
1 × 284 mL	1 × 10 oz.	Condensed beef consommé	
8	8	Hamburger buns, split and toasted	Spoon over buns. Serves 8.

People Napkins

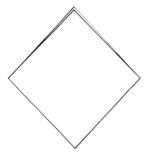

1. Begin with white or pastel plain paper napkins. Place with open corners pointing up.

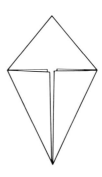

2. Fold left and right corners over so sides meet from top corner downward

Porky Pops

May be cooked ahead and reheated.

1	1	Large egg	Beat first 7 ingredients
1 mL	¼ tsp.	Onion powder	together in small bowl
5 mL	1 tsp.	Salt	until frothy.
1 mL	¼ tsp.	Pepper	
1 mL	¼ tsp.	Oregano	
1 mL	¼ tsp.	Garlic powder	
1 mL	¼ tsp.	Thyme	
454 g	1 lb.	Lean ground pork	Mix in pork. Divide in 4 equal parts. From each part, shape 2 rectangular cubes.
8	8	Popsicle sticks	Insert popsicle stick in center of each. Sprinkle with paprika.
		Paprika, sprinkle	Arrange on baking tray. Cook in 350°F (175°C) oven for 30 minutes until no pink remains in pork. Makes 8.

Pictured on page 39.

3. Turn over. Draw face of girl for girls.

4. Draw face of boy for boys.

Coleslaw *A make-ahead slaw.*

1 L	4 cups	Grated cabbage, packed	Combine cabbage, bean
1	1	Large handful of bean sprouts	sprouts and apple in large bowl.
1	1	Grated peeled apple	

Dressing

250 mL	1 cup	Salad dressing (or mayonnaise	Stir all 6 ingredients well. Add to cabbage mixture. Toss. To make this ahead, chill cab-
50 mL	3 tbsp.	Milk	bage and bean sprouts
15 mL	1 tbsp.	Granulated sugar	together. Add apple to
10 mL	2 tsp.	Vinegar	dressing so it won't darken.
2 mL	½ tsp.	Onion powder	Combine shortly before
1 mL	¼ tsp.	Celery salt	serving. Serves 8.

1. **Cheese Finery page 58**
2. **Egg Ribbons page 74**
3. **Cheese Triangles page 63**
4. **Spiced Nuts page 68**
5. **Ham Pinwheels page 73**
6. **Crunchy Crisps page 61**

Dishes Courtesy Of:
Call The Kettle Black

Tiered Stand Courtesy Of:
Le Gnome

Cocktail Party

Guests: This type of party is usually for a crowd. Most often there are more guests than chairs. People stand, mill around, visit, eat, sip drinks and continue visiting. Set the time on invitations near the dinner hour, such as 5:00 to 7:00, 4:30 to 7:00 or 4:30 to 7:30. Your may want to ask for an RSVP on the invitation. It is a good idea to advise if you have a no smoking home, by indicating guests may smoke on the patio.

A cocktail party is a great way to start off a long evening. Invite a small group for a short spell before attending a larger function. Keep nibblies and drinks to a minimum.

Menu Planning: Variety is definitely the spice of life at such a party. Cheese, crudités, meats, seafood, fruit and pastries are in order. Set out cold appetizers. Put out smaller quantities of hot appetizers and keep refilling from the oven or microwave. Remember, a large platter of two or three kinds is more impressive than only one kind. However, a smaller tray or dish full of one appetizer will whet any appetite! Replenish dips often, so bowls are always at least half full. Individual plates are not necessary but cocktail napkins are a must. Food should be easy to handle and eaten in one or two bites. Allow about eight pieces per person. If you feel most guests will have a supper of nibblies, allow more. In that case, small plates would be convenient.

Have extra glasses on hand. Supply coffee and at least one non-alcoholic cold drink/punch for non drinkers. The hostess/host should invite guests to help themselves at a do-it-yourself bar. Allow three or four drinks per person just to be sure you have enough.

Room Setting: If necessary, move some of the furniture to allow more space to mingle. Cast an eye around the room. Remove breakable objects that could be bumped into because of crowding. Also, be aware of "traffic jams" and entice people to move around. Put coasters everywhere. Set out food in one or more locations along with paper cocktail napkins and containers to hold discarded wooden picks. Set up more than one bar if you have room. Limit cocktails to two or three kinds.

One To Three Weeks Prior: Send invitations. Plan menu by categories — hot and cold, meat, fish and veggies, sweet and savory, spicy and mild. Make appetizers to freeze. Stock up on drink supplies. Stock up on mixes. Make ice cubes.

One To Two Days Prior: Arrange furniture. Set up bar. Set up food areas. Do final grocery shopping. Buy extra cheese and crackers just in case there are extra guests or extra hungry guests.

One Day Prior: Transfer freezer food to refrigerator. Chill mixes. Buy flowers including one, two or three for a bud vase for each bathroom.

Day Of Party: Decide where to put coats. Supply hangers if needed. Place fresh towels in the bathroom. Check tissues. Ask your spouse or a friend to share the hosting so that one of you can answer the door, introduce everyone and keep them mingling. The other hostess/host can take care of the food.

Special Touches: Hang a sign by the doorbell, "Welcome, Come In". Choose mood setting music — light, instrumental.

Spinach Canapés   *Short little stacks.*

Base

		Pastry, your own or a mix, enough for 2 crusts

Roll pastry ⅛ inch (3 mm) thick. Cut into 1¾ inch (4.5 cm) rounds. Arrange on baking sheet. Bake in 400°F (205°C) oven 10 to 12 minutes until golden.

Filling

7	7	Cooked ham slices
284 g	10 oz.	Frozen chopped spinach, thawed, squeezed dry
		Salt, sprinkle
		Pepper, sprinkle

Cut ham in same sized circles to fit over baked pastry rounds. Put ½ tsp.(2 mL) spinach over ham. Sprinkle with salt and pepper. There will be spinach left over.

Topping

60 mL	¼ cup	Sour cream
60 mL	¼ cup	Salad dressing (or mayonnaise)
125 mL	½ cup	Grated medium Cheddar cheese
1 mL	¼ tsp.	Onion powder

Pictured on page 57.

Combine sour cream, salad dressing, cheese and onion powder in small bowl. Spread 1 tsp. (5 mL) over each spinach covered round. Arrange on ungreased tray. Broil about 4 inches (10 cm) from heat until hot and melted. Makes 28.

Variation: Use grated Mozzarella cheese instead of Cheddar for a white topping.

1. **Denver Canapés page 57**
2. **Spinach Canapés page 56**

Platter Courtesy Of:
Le Gnome

Denver Canapés

Make these the same day as you plan to serve them.

75 mL	⅓ **cup**	Finely chopped onion	Sauté onion and green pepper in butter until soft.
75 mL	⅓ **cup**	Finely chopped green pepper	
15 mL	**1 tbsp.**	Butter or margarine	
6	6	Large eggs	Beat eggs in bowl until frothy. Add next 6 ingredients. Add onion mixture. Stir. Pour into greased 9 x 13 inch (22 x 33 cm) pan. Bake in 350°F (175°C) oven for about 15 minutes until firm. Cut into 54 squares.
75 mL	⅓ **cup**	Milk	
75 mL	⅓ **cup**	Salad dressing (or mayonnaise)	
175 mL	¾ **cup**	Chopped ham	
30 mL	**2 tbsp.**	Chopped pimiento	
1 mL	¼ **tsp.**	Salt	
		Pepper, sprinkle	
14	14	Bread slices, toasted, buttered, crusts removed, cut in 4 squares	Place egg square on toast. Garnish with pimiento pieces. Serve warm or cool. Cover if reheating. Makes 54.
		Pimiento pieces	

Pictured below.

Cheese Finery
You can make these ahead and chill or freeze.

50 mL	3 tbsp.	Salad dressing (or mayonnaise)	Mix first 5 ingredients in bowl.
450 mL	2 cups	Grated sharp Cheddar cheese	
128 mL	4½ oz.	Chopped pimiento plus juice	
2 mL	½ tsp.	Onion powder	
0.5 mL	⅛ tsp.	Hot pepper sauce	
16	16	Brown bread slices, day old	Cut 3 circles 1¾ inch (4.5 cm) from each bread slice. Sandwich brown and white circles with filling. Arrange on serving plate with some brown sides up as well as some white. Makes 48.
16	16	White bread slices, day old	
		Butter or margarine, softened	
		Stuffed olive slices	

Pictured on page 53.

Flat Orange Cakes

Similar to a fried biscuit.

500 mL	2 cups	All-purpose flour	Combine first 5 ingredients in medium bowl. Cut in butter until crumbly.
75 mL	⅓ cup	Granulated sugar	
5 mL	1 tsp.	Baking powder	
1 mL	¼ tsp.	Salt	
5 mL	1 tsp.	Grated orange rind	
125 mL	½ cup	Butter or margarine	
1	1	Large egg, lightly beaten	Add egg and orange juice. Stir, then mix with hands until ball of dough forms. Roll ¼ inch (6 mm) thick on lightly floured surface. Cut into 2 or 3 inch (5 or 7 cm) rounds. Fry in frying pan over medium-low heat about 1½ minutes per side, browning both sides. Serve cold. Set out orange marmalade to spread. Makes 2 or 3 dozen.
30 mL	2 tbsp.	Prepared orange juice	

Pictured on this page.

Platter And Bowl Set Courtesy Of:
Bukoba Fine Teas And Coffees

Creamy Meatballs

Have these in the refrigerator ready to heat in a jiffy.

454 g	1 lb.	Lean ground beef
125 mL	½ cup	Dry bread crumbs
125 mL	½ cup	Milk or water
1	1	Large egg
15 mL	1 tbsp.	Onion flakes
5 mL	1 tsp.	Worcestershire sauce
4 mL	¾ tsp.	Salt
1 mL	¼ tsp.	Pepper

Combine first 8 ingredients in bowl. Mix. Shape into 1 inch (2.5 cm) balls. Arrange on baking sheet. Cook in 350°F (175°C) oven for 15 minutes until done (or brown in greased frying pan).

284 mL	10 oz.	Condensed cream of mushroom soup
250 g	8 oz.	Cream cheese, softened
125 mL	½ cup	Water
1 mL	¼ tsp.	Paprika

Heat and stir remaining 4 ingredients In large heavy saucepan until smooth. Add meatballs. Serve in chafing dish. Makes 5½ dozen.

Perk A Punch

This is heated in a coffee percolator. Aroma is great!

1 L	4½ cups	Prepared orange juice
1 L	4½ cups	Unsweetened pineapple juice
500 mL	2¼ cups	Water
0.5 mL	⅛ tsp.	Salt

Measure first 4 ingredients into coffee percolator.

11 mL	2¼ tsp.	Whole cloves
1	1	Cinnamon stick, broken up
175 mL	¾ cup	Brown sugar, packed

Place cloves, cinnamon stick and brown sugar in coffee basket. Run through perk cycle. Makes 11 cups (2.5 L).

Pictured on page 61.

Crunchy Crisps   *Crunchy and cheesy little bits.*

125 mL	½ cup	Butter or margarine, softened	Mix butter, cheese, hot pepper sauce and salt in bowl.
250 mL	1 cup	Grated sharp Cheddar cheese	
1 mL	¼ tsp.	Hot pepper sauce	
0.5 mL	⅛ tsp.	Salt	
250 mL	1 cup	All-purpose flour	Add flour and cereal. Stir. Work with hands. Shape into walnut size balls. Arrange on ungreased baking sheet. Press down with fork. Bake in 350°F (175°C) oven for about 15 to 20 minutes until lightly browned. Cool. Makes about 36.
250 mL	1 cup	Crisp rice cereal	

Pictured on page 53.

Perk A Punch page 60

Mug Set Courtesy Of:
Le Gnome

Fruit Dip
Have dip and fruit chilled until needed.

350 mL	1½ cups	Sour cream
60 mL	¼ cup	Salad dressing (or mayonnaise
60 mL	¼ cup	Brown sugar, packed
75 mL	⅓ cup	Chopped raisins
1 mL	¼ tsp.	Rum flavoring

Combine first 5 ingredients in bowl. Stir well. Chill until needed. Makes 2 cups (450 mL) dip.

Assorted fruit
Strawberries, cantaloupe, grapes, banana, apple, pineapple

Serve with assorted fruit which has been cut into bite size pieces. Dip apple and banana in lemon juice to keep from browning.

❶   ❷   ❸

Cheese Triangles *Good hot or cold. Fancy.*

1	1	Large egg	Beat egg in small mixing bowl until frothy. Add all 3 cheeses and parsley. Beat until smooth.
125 g	4 oz.	Cream cheese, softened	
250 g	8 oz.	Feta cheese, crumbled	
30 mL	2 tbsp.	Grated Parmesan cheese	
5 mL	1 tsp.	Parsley flakes	

454 g   1 lb.   Phyllo pastry

250 mL   1 cup   Butter or margarine, melted and warm

Lay 1 sheet of phyllo on working surface. Work quickly. Cover remainder with damp cloth. ❶ Brush sheet generously with melted butter. Cut into strips 4 inches (10 cm) wide. ❷ Fold each strip in half lengthwise to make 2 inches (5 cm) wide. Brush with butter. ❸ Place 1 tsp. (5 mL) filling in center at one end. Fold 1 corner over to form triangle. ❹ Continue folding over in same fashion to end of strip. Brush final triangle with butter. Place on baking sheet. Repeat. Bake in 400°F (205°C) oven for about 15 minutes until golden. Makes 5½ dozen.

④

Cheese Triangles

Pictured on page 53.

Vegetable Dip

Good tangy make-ahead dip. A very slight hint of curry.

500 mL	2 cups	Salad dressing (or mayonnaise)
50 mL	3 tbsp.	Ketchup
5 mL	1 tsp.	Worcestershire sauce
2 mL	½ tsp.	Garlic powder
2 mL	½ tsp.	Onion salt
2 mL	½ tsp.	Curry powder

Combine first 6 ingredients in bowl. Stir. A bit of milk may be added if too thick. Chill. Makes a generous 2 cups (500 mL) dip.

Assorted raw vegetables

Green and red pepper sticks, carrot sticks, asparagus tips, cauliflower, broccoli, mushrooms, celery, zucchini, radish

Serve with assorted vegetables.

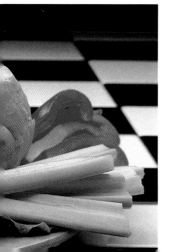

Spinach Dip

This makes a large amount but don't be concerned, you'll need it. It's great.

284 g	10 oz.	Frozen chopped spinach, thawed, squeezed dry	Place first 4 ingredients in blender. Process until smooth. Turn into bowl.
250 mL	1 cup	Salad dressing (or mayonnaise)	
250 mL	1 cup	Sour cream	
125 mL	½ cup	Chopped onion	
1 x 45 g	1 x 1½ oz.	Envelope vegetable soup mix	Stir in vegetable soup mix and water chestnuts. Cover. Chill for at least 2 hours. Makes 3¾ cups (875 mL).
284 mL	10 oz.	Canned chopped water chestnuts, drained	
		Round bread loaf, hollowed out	Fill bread loaf with dip. Serve with vegetables, bread chunks and crackers. This may also be wrapped in foil and heated in 300°F (150°C) oven for 2 to 3 hours.
		Assorted raw vegetables	
		Bread chunks and crackers	

Spinach Dip

Tray Courtesy Of:
Ikea

Mini Pizzas *Cups of pizza.*

Pizza Crust

250 mL	1 cup	Warm water	In large warm bowl, combine water, butter and salt. Stir to melt butter.
30 mL	2 tbsp	Butter or margarine	
2 mL	½ tsp.	Salt	

750 mL	3 cups	All-purpose flour	Stir in flour and yeast. Add a bit more flour if necessary, just until it is a soft dough and not too sticky. Knead on floured surface until smooth. Place in greased bowl turning once so top is greased. Cover. Let rise until double in bulk about 45 to 60 minutes.
1 × 8 g	1 × ⅓ oz.	Instant yeast	

Pizza Sauce

15 mL	1 tbsp.	Butter or margarine	As soon as dough is put to rise, begin the sauce. Heat butter in large saucepan. Add onion. Sauté until soft.
1	1	Small onion, coarsely chopped	

Continued on next page.

540 mL	19 oz.	Canned tomatoes
1	1	Bay leaf
5 mL	1 tsp.	Granulated sugar
5 mL	1 tsp.	Salt
2 mL	½ tsp.	Oregano
		Pepper, light sprinkle

Add tomatoes, bay leaf, sugar, salt, oregano and pepper. Bring to a boil. Cover. Cook slowly for about 30 minutes stirring occasionally until sauce has thickened slightly. Discard bay leaf. Remove from heat. Makes 2¼ cups (500 mL).

30 mL	2 tbsp.	Cooking oil
30 mL	2 tbsp.	Grated Parmesan cheese
150 mL	⅔ cup	Prepared pizza sauce
125 g	¼ lb.	Cooked ham, thinly sliced, chopped
150 mL	⅔ cup	Grated mozzarella cheese

Punch dough down. Roll a portion fairly thin. Cut into 2½ inch (6 cm) circles. Line greased tiny 1½ inch (4 cm) tart pans. Pierce bottoms with fork in 2 or 3 places. Brush shells with cooking oil. Sprinkle bottoms with ⅛ tsp. (0.5 mL) Parmesan cheese. Add in order ½ tsp. (2 mL) each of pizza sauce, chopped ham and moz-zarella cheese. Bake in 450°C (230°C) oven for about 10 minutes until crust is lightly browned. Reheat in 350°F (175°C) oven for 5 to 10 minutes until hot. These freeze well. Makes 5 dozen.

Pictured on page 69.

Spiced Nuts

Make lots of these days before you need them.

1	1	Egg white (large), room temperature	Beat egg white and water in small mixing bowl until smooth consistency.
10 mL	2 tsp.	Water	
500 mL	2 cups	Mixed nuts or salted peanuts	Stir in mixed nuts.
125 mL	½ cup	Granulated sugar	Mix next 5 ingredients in small bowl. Add to nuts. Stir to coat. Spread on greased baking sheet. Bake in 250°F (120°C) oven for 1 hour, stirring nuts every 15 minutes. Store in covered container or freeze. Makes 2 cups (500 mL).
5 mL	1 tsp.	Cinnamon	
2 mL	½ tsp.	Nutmeg	
1 mL	¼ tsp.	Ginger	
0.5 mL	⅛ tsp.	Salt	

Pictured on page 53.

1. Mini Pizzas page 66
2. Hot Bread Puffs page 7
3. Hash Pastries page 70

Glass Tray Courtesy Of:
Le Gnome

Hash Pastries *These look like little puffy pillows.*

Hash Filling

15 mL	1 tbsp.	Cooking oil	Heat cooking oil in frying pan. Add onion, green pepper, celery and ground beef. Sauté until browned and soft.
250 mL	1 cup	Chopped onion	
60 mL	¼ cup	Chopped green pepper	
60 mL	¼ cup	Chopped celery	
250 g	½ lb.	Lean ground beef	
15 mL	1 tbsp.	All-purpose flour	Mix in flour. Add water. Stir until it comes to a boil and thickens.
125 mL	½ cup	Water	
125 mL	½ cup	Instant rice	Add rice, bouillon powder, ketchup and salt. Stir. Let stand 5 minutes. Cool well. Makes a scant 2 cups (450 mL).
10 mL	2 tsp.	Beef bouillon powder	
30 mL	2 tbsp.	Ketchup	
2 mL	½ tsp.	Salt	
2 x 397 g	2 x 14 oz.	Frozen puff pastry, thawed	Roll pastry fairly thin. Cut into 2 inch (5 cm) squares. Put 1 tsp. (5 mL) filling in center. Dampen edges. Cover with second pastry square. Press with fork to seal. Cut slit in top. Arrange on ungreased baking sheet. Bake in 400°F (205 °C) oven for 10 to 15 minutes until browned. Makes about 7½ dozen.

Pictured on page 69.

Hot Bread Puffs

*Cheese coated cubes are bites of bliss.
Recipe may be halved.*

1	1	Unsliced bread loaf, crust removed	Cut bread into 1 inch (2.5 cm) cubes. These are easier to dip if partially frozen.
250 mL	1 cup	Butter or margarine	Combine next 4 ingredients in double boiler. Stir often as it melts. Remove from heat.
250 g	8 oz.	Cream cheese	
750 mL	3 cups	Grated sharp Cheddar cheese	
10 mL	2 tsp.	Worcestershire sauce	
4	4	Egg whites (large), room temperature	Beat egg whites in small mixing bowl until stiff. Fold into hot mixture. Pierce frozen or partially frozen bread cubes with fork. Dip into hot mixture to coat. Transfer to ungreased baking sheet. Chill all day or over night. Bake in 400°F (205°C) oven for about 10 minutes until lightly browned. To keep on hand, freeze on tray. Store in plastic container or bag. Thaw before cooking. Makes about 120.

Pictured on page 69.

Turtle Brownies

A great treat containing chocolate, caramel and nuts.

500 g	17 oz.	Bag of caramels	Melt caramels in first amount of milk in double boiler or heavy saucepan.
75 mL	⅓ cup	Evaporated milk	
1	1	Chocolate cake mix, 2 layer size	Combine next 4 ingredients in bowl. Mix. Press ½ mixture into ungreased 9 x 13 inch (22 x 33 cm) pan. Bake in 350°F (175°C) oven for 6 minutes.
175 mL	¾ cup	Butter or margarine, melted	
75 mL	⅓ cup	Evaporated milk	
250 mL	1 cup	Chopped walnuts	
250 mL	1 cup	Semisweet chocolate chips	Sprinkle chocolate chips evenly over top. Pour caramel mixture over chips. Carefully spoon remaining cake mixture over all. Spread evenly. Return to oven. Bake 15 to 18 minutes more. Cool several hours. Cuts into 54 squares.

Pictured below.

Ham Pinwheels
Make one day ahead or make and freeze ahead.

Metric	Imperial	Ingredient	Method
1 × 184 g	1 × 6.5 oz.	Canned ham flakes	Mash first 5 ingredients together with fork.
50 mL	3 tbsp.	Salad dressing (or mayonnaise)	
15 mL	1 tbsp.	Worcestershire sauce	
5 mL	1 tsp.	Prepared mustard	
1 mL	¼ tsp.	Onion powder	
1	1	White unsliced bread loaf, day old, sliced lengthwise Butter or margarine, softened Gherkins	Remove crust from 3 long slices of bread. Roll lightly with rolling pin. Spread to edge with butter. Spread to edge with ham mixture. Arrange gherkins end to end along short end. Roll up. Place seam side down in container. Cover with damp tea towel. Chill. Slice thinly to serve. Makes 12 slices per roll, a total of 36.

Pictured on page 53.

Egg Ribbons

This filling is enjoyed by all.

6	6	Large hard-boiled eggs, chopped	Mix first 6 ingredients in bowl.
60 mL	¼ cup	Finely diced celery	
60 mL	¼ cup	Salad dressing (or mayonnaise)	
30 mL	2 tbsp.	Sweet pickle relish	
2 mL	½ tsp.	Salt	
1 mL	¼ tsp.	Onion powder	
8	8	Dark bread slices, day old	Use 2 dark and 1 white slice per stack. Place dark slice on bottom and top. Butter and spread filling between each slice. Cut off crusts. Repeat. Wrap and chill. To serve, cut into ½ inch (12 mm) slices. Cut each slice into 3 or 4 strips. Makes about 4 dozen.
4	4	White bread slices, day old	
		Butter or margarine, softened	

Pictured on page 53.

Measurement Tables

Throughout this book measurements are given in Conventional and Metric measure. To compensate for differences between the two measurements due to rounding, a full metric measure is not always used. The cup used is the standard 8 fluid ounce. Temperature is given in degrees Fahrenheit and Celsius. Baking pan measurements are in inches and centimetres. An exact metric conversion is given below as well as the working equivalent (Standard Measure).

SPOONS

Conventional Measure	Metric Exact Conversion Millilitre (mL)	Metric Standard Measure Millilitre (mL)
$1/8$ teaspoon (tsp.)	0.6 mL	0.5 mL
$1/4$ teaspoon (tsp.)	1.2 mL	1 mL
$1/2$ teaspoon (tsp.)	2.4 mL	2 mL
1 teaspoon (tsp.)	4.7 mL	5 mL
2 teaspoons (tsp.)	9.4 mL	10 mL
1 tablespoon (tbsp.)	14.2 mL	15 mL

CUPS

$1/4$ cup (4 tbsp.)	56.8 mL	50 mL
$1/3$ cup ($5^1/3$ tbsp.)	75.6 mL	75 mL
$1/2$ cup (8 tbsp.)	113.7 mL	125 mL
$2/3$ cup ($10^2/3$ tbsp.)	151.2 mL	150 mL
$3/4$ cup (12 tbsp.)	170.5 mL	175 mL
1 cup (16 tbsp.)	227.3 mL	250 mL
$4^1/2$ cups	1022.9 mL	1000 mL (1 L)

CASSEROLES (Canada & Britain)

Standard Size Casserole	Exact Metric Measure
1 qt. (5 cups)	1.13 L
$1^1/2$ qts. ($7^1/2$ cups)	1.69 L
2 qts. (10 cups)	2.25 L
$2^1/2$ qts. ($12^1/2$ cups)	2.81 L
3 qts. (15 cups)	3.38 L
4 qts. (20 cups)	4.5 L
5 qts. (25 cups)	5.63 L

CASSEROLES (United States)

Standard Size Casserole	Exact Metric Measure
1 qt. (4 cups)	900 mL
$1^1/2$ qts. (6 cups)	1.35 L
2 qts. (8 cups)	1.8 L
$2^1/2$ qts. (10 cups)	2.25 L
3 qts. (12 cups)	2.7 L
4 qts. (16 cups)	3.6 L
5 qts. (20 cups)	4.5 L

DRY MEASUREMENTS

Conventional Measure Ounces (oz.)	Exact Conversion Grams (g)	Standard Measure Grams (g)
1 oz.	28.3 g	30 g
2 oz.	56.7 g	55 g
3 oz.	85.0 g	85 g
4 oz.	113.4 g	125 g
5 oz.	141.7 g	140 g
6 oz.	170.1 g	170 g
7 oz.	198.4 g	200 g
8 oz.	226.8 g	250 g
16 oz.	453.6 g	500 g
32 oz.	907.2 g	1000 g (1 kg)

PANS

Conventional Inches	Metric Centimetres
8x8 inch	20x20 cm
9x9 inch	22x22 cm
9x13 inch	22x33 cm
10x15 inch	25x38 cm
11x17 inch	28x43 cm
8x2 inch round	20x5 cm
9x2 inch round	22x5 cm
10x4$1/2$ inch tube	25x11 cm
8x4x3 inch loaf	20x10x7 cm
9x5x3 inch loaf	22x12x7 cm

OVEN TEMPERATURES

Fahrenheit (°F)	Celsius (°C)
175°	80°
200°	95°
225°	110°
250°	120°
275°	140°
300°	150°
325°	160°
350°	175°
375°	190°
400°	205°
425°	220°
450°	230°
475°	240°
500°	260°

Index

MAIL ORDER FORM
Deduct $5.00 for every $35.00 ordered

Save $5.00

COMPANY'S COMING SERIES

Quantity		Quantity		Quantity	
	150 Delicious Squares		Vegetables		Microwave Cooking
	Casseroles		Main Courses		Preserves
	Muffins & More		Pasta		Light Casseroles
	Salads		Cakes		Chicken, Etc.
	Appetizers		Barbecues		Kids Cooking
	Desserts		Dinners of the World		Fish & Seafood
	Soups & Sandwiches		Lunches		Breads
	Holiday Entertaining		Pies		Meatless Cooking (April 1997)
	Cookies		Light Recipes		

	NO. OF BOOKS	PRICE
FIRST BOOK: $12.99 + $3.00 shipping = **$15.99 each** x		= $
ADDITIONAL BOOKS: $12.99 + $1.50 shipping = **$14.49 each** x		= $

PINT SIZE BOOKS

Quantity		Quantity		Quantity	
	Finger Food		Buffets		Chocolate
	Party Planning		Baking Delights		

	NO. OF BOOKS	PRICE
FIRST BOOK: $4.99 + $2.00 shipping = **$6.99 each** x		= $
ADDITIONAL BOOKS: $4.99 + $1.00 shipping = **$5.99 each** x		= $

- **MAKE CHEQUE OR MONEY ORDER PAYABLE TO:** *COMPANY'S COMING PUBLISHING LIMITED*
- **ORDERS OUTSIDE CANADA:** *Must be paid in U.S. funds by cheque or money order drawn on Canadian or U.S. bank.*
- *Prices subject to change without prior notice.*
- *Sorry, no C.O.D.'s*

TOTAL PRICE FOR ALL BOOKS	$
Less $5.00 for every $35.00 ordered —	$
SUBTOTAL	$
Canadian residents add G.S.T. +	$
TOTAL AMOUNT ENCLOSED	$

Please complete shipping address on reverse.

Gift Giving

- Let us help you with your gift giving!
- We will send cookbooks directly to the recipients of your choice if you give us their names and addresses.
- Be sure to specify the titles you wish to send to each person.
- If you would like to include your personal note or card, we will be pleased to enclose it with your gift order.
- Company's Coming Cookbooks make excellent gifts. Birthdays, bridal showers, Mother's Day, Father's Day, graduation or any occasion... collect them all!

Shipping address

Send the Company's Coming Cookbooks listed on the reverse side of this coupon, to:

Name:

Street:

City: Province/State:

Postal Code/Zip: Tel: (   )   —

Company's Coming Publishing Limited
Box 8037, Station F
Edmonton, Alberta, Canada T6H 4N9
Tel: (403) 450-6223
Fax: (403) 450-1857